GHOST STORIES
Reflections of the Heart and Mind

AUTUMN ZALOUMIS

Ghost stories: reflections of the heart and mind
© Autumn Zaloumis 2017

Images from bigstock.com

All rights reserved. No part of this publication may be reproduced, stored in a retrieval system, or transmitted in any form or by any means, electronic, mechanical, photocopying, recording or otherwise, without the prior written permission of the author.

National Library of Australia Cataloguing-in-Publication entry (pbk)

Creator:	Zaloumis, Autumn, author.
Title:	Ghost stories: reflections of the heart and mind / Autumn Zaloumis.
ISBN:	9781925680126 (paperback)
	9781925680133 (eBook)
Subjects:	Poetry.
	Australian poetry--21st century.

Published by Autumn Zaloumis and Ocean Reeve Publishing
www.oceanreeve.com

OCEAN REEVE PUBLISHING

Contents

About The Author v
Foreword vii
Introduction ix

"But I wait for you" 1
"Carnal" 2
"Asleep" 4
"Words" 6
"Dear Man" 8
"Mateo open dialogue" 10
"Diseased Poetry" 12
"Sharp Words" 14
"I sit in silence" 16
"Mr Redding and Miss Glenda Devine" 18
"Me and my Pride" 19
"Man" 20
"Human" 21
"Nights (Old Age)" 22
"Stars together" 23
"You" 24
"Second Chance" 26
"Hibernation" 27
"Pride Part 2" 28

"Oh yeah"..................................29
"Hung out to dry"...........................30
"Hello, Stranger"............................32
"Kiss kiss".................................33
"Sweet spot"...............................34
"Shepherd".................................37
"Dear Elena"...............................38
"Every smell I smell him"....................41
"Sweet solitude"............................42
"Take me to your river".....................43
"Perception"...............................44
"How I love Love"..........................49
"Thoughts"................................51
"Daddy, put my soul to rest"................52

About The Author

Autumn Zaloumis is writer based on the Gold Coast. At eleven years old, she began writing as a creative outlet, loving how the play of words depicted the harmony of art and expressed subjects impressed deeply on her heart. From the age of sixteen, she explored the different facets of love and compiled it all into her first book. As the years passed and her writing and perspective evolved, she reworked her writings into poetry and now presents that book to the world.

Foreword

There was a time in my career when I was told 'no-one reads poetry anymore'. I remember looking at that person with sadness thinking it was unfortunate they didn't have the relationship with the written word as I did. For years I admired and enjoyed the works of Walt Whitman, John Keats, T.S. Elliot and Lord Alfred Tennyson. To think there would be no one else who understood the power of the poet and articulate a thought, feeling, experience in prose was unfathomable. At the time my role was as a sales representative for a traditional publishing house and I had the privilege of promoting and marketing some traditional poetry compilations into trade stores. It was always a delight to see bookshop store owners and managers open the poetry books and read the written picture in front of them. Over the years to come, poetry became sporadic. I didn't see it as much as I did in the early 2000's and the styles were eclectic and diverse. There was nothing new that had that same emotional connection that the more traditional poetry did, or at least the poetry I worked with. Then came Ghost Stories.

    I met Autumn Zaloumis a few years ago as she was enquiring about the publishing process, and at the time I could see she had this desire to express herself creatively, but it wasn't apparent as to how that creativity would take form. In mid-2017, following Autumn's return from a trip to Africa, she sent through an urgent need to publish. She was desperate to get something down after such a long wait. I soon discovered her amazing ability to open her mind and heart for all to see through beautifully written poetry.

With such heart, I found her poetry to be very similar to the way the older poets made me feel. It wasn't just the odd one or two, poem after poem resonated and caused me to reflect and explore my own relationship with love, relationships, and emotions. Now with a 30+ collection of poetry, Autumn shares her retrospective soul and contemplative heart in this deep and often revealing collection. As you are about to see, Autumn also has an amazing talent in articulating her emotions into words and an unbounded creative future.

It was an honour to be asked to write this foreword, but a greater honour is now, finally, to see Autumn published and sharing her creativity with the world.

Ocean Reeve
Author Coach/Mentor

Introduction

The title piece for this array of poems is *Ghost Stories*.

When I hear the phrase "Ghost Stories", I'm immediately drawn to a bonfire, friends and a hell of a good story. Warmed and frightened at the same time, I wonder, could this story be true? Does Big Foot really exist? Or is it too good to be true?

Ghost Stories is just like that. Come cuddle up next to a poetic bonfire. This collection of thoughts crept out from the dark corners of my mind and heart—everything, from hidden love, celestial workings and truth.

Read all that is loud on the walls of a heart heard in the darkness never spoken.

A gesture to the universe and all its discomfort, bliss and euphoria.

Written for all my lovers—human, inhuman, celestial, present and future.

"But I wait for you"

I see the crease below your eye—
Just above it is an ageing nirvana.
In twenty years, I'm going to keep writing about you,
The tale will be called:
Love: My old man and me.
You look at me and I look at you—
What would they say about such a pair?
Dancing fools on the floor?
Drunks who want some more?
Music whores?
The girl who didn't know what to do,
The boy who was never really there.
Together they ventured near and far.
Was he in love?
She was . . .
Some things are better left unsaid.
I hope one day you read this instead—
My words left unspoken
I release them from my thoughts onto paper,
Recorded
So you know it was true.
Maybe it will make its way to you
And, perchance, you'd feel the same way too.

"Carnal"

Miles are carnal when I'm left with idle thoughts of you,
Somehow, strangely, you've left a piece of yourself within me.
You've made a home to stay.
So naturally your memory remains.
Remnants of a figure lingers,
Spiritually present, aching insomnia—
No matter the equation I rely on, it brings me back to you.
The only solution I'm left with is no sleep.
The next day, misery—
Walking aimlessly, tiredly, I'll pretend
I'm over you and go about my day-to-day.
And just when I think I've fooled myself,
A song that reminds me of you rises to the surface
Just lingering enough to make me realise I'm nothing but a liar
Manifesting into a girl.
Then when I hear just about every song that reminds me of you,
I realise I'm nothing but a liar
Caught up in a dream.
Nothing but a liar, hoping you and I manifest into something more.

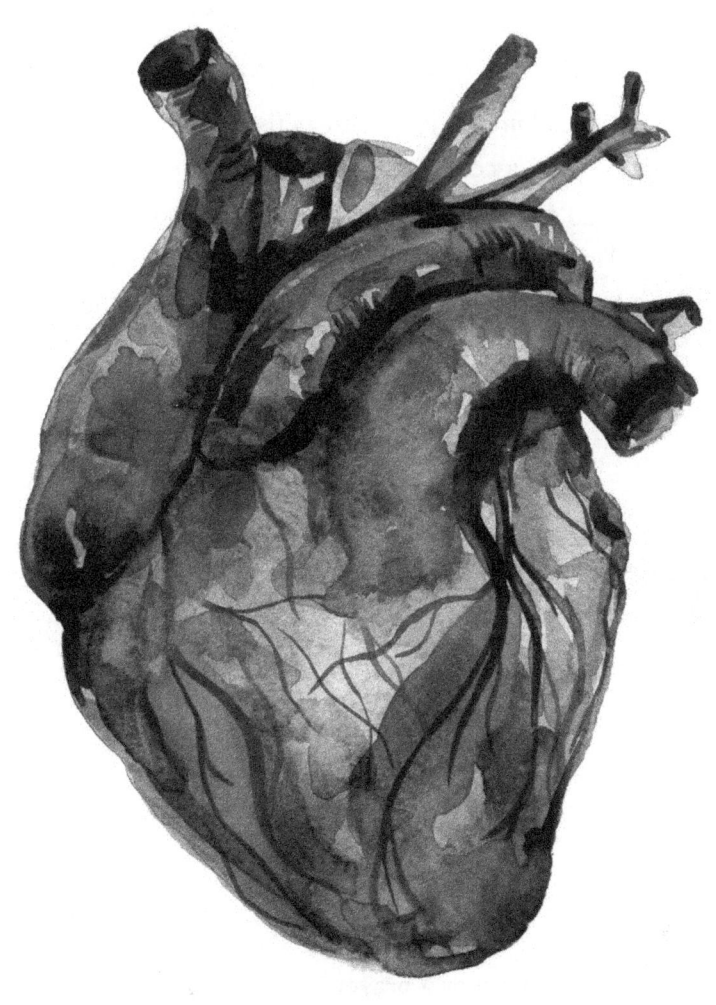

"Asleep"

I fell asleep.
Head in harmony with all that you are.
On a couch, quite uncomfortable.
I concede that my night is over and
Time and time again my thoughts interrupt
Rest, but I rest in the thought of whatever becomes of
you and me.
Like a magnet of desire
I'm sure I cannot contain much more of you,
And as you do
Your lips meet my forehead
And awakening to my dreamland
Where I wish to see you—
Could it be our future remains as simple as this?
I've never wanted a whole lot
Just three
Love, Faith and Happiness.
I'm convinced you're all three.

I sit on the sandy shore
Whisper a prayer into the sky
It carries a promise on the night wind
Just me and my God.

I told my daddy about a boy:
He has the greatest smile, I swear.
Every time I see it, he uses it against me
Every time he uses it, I want the ground to swallow me.
Magnet of desire, my heart is in harmony with all that you are.
He uses all his fibres against me—
His eyes entice me to have the ground swallow me.

"Words"

You've helped depict the most difficult parts of me.
The things I can't say.
Everything about you is beautiful—
An outlet of relief, my soul,
My core, everything that will remain true.
I never thought it could be you fastened to my everything,
my whole life.
You were the beginning and will see my end;
You take form, breathe creation
Piece by piece, envelope signed, sealed and delivered.
I thank you.
A poem for my poems.
I pray we stay forever entwined,
Forever reading, forever growing and forever falling in love.

"Dear Man"

Admirer of heights within mountains
Fearless explorer in mighty seas
Fishermen of tides and universal circuits
A mystery not even opened within themselves

Strength lies in the bones of a sculptured Adam,
Provider and enchanter. 2017 has a new destiny for you:
Equal and de-masculinised side chick

What is history to write about you?
Feminism accumulates your status more and more each day—
To be equally yoked,
A conquest of feminine women.
What happens when the man gains breasts?

What is left to plough and what is expected?
Times are changing and so are you.
The earth, rich with conquests,
The veins of a warrior not limited by status and what is supposed to be.

Visionary of visions, tap in and see all that can be.
With the confidence of a giant killer, slay giants—
and when you're tempted to fight the tears,
Release them.

Words of affirmation,
Here are yours:

Respecter of my person, you are loved.
Leader of intricate dimensions that surround a woman's
heart, you are saluted.
Provider of all things that shelter with bare hands and
even greater courage, I applaud you.

Creative creator, no other species has a mind like yours.
The earth, if full of the very things that are beneficial and
magical—
Emotional rock—

Your countenance of a man not moved by emotions,
though frustrating, is logical.
You think ahead and remain steadfast
in all that is best.

Lover, warmth and embracer of all things lonely,
Counterpart of all dreams come true, I thank you.
Best friend of all life's adventures and distant old age.

"Mateo open dialogue"

He tries to catch me
Forever using *please, slow down*
Reassurances that it's okay
What then? All that is me reaches daily ends

Anxiety
Always in a rush
Movements to keep one's heart racing
Persuaded by fear
Losing all consciousness, bar
Trying to create a vision in loss of self
Him trying to change a destiny that has left peace
One piece left of me
Nothing to give you
Path of disaster inflicted on self

Mateo
Calm down, don't lose peace
That which is yours will find you
Walk in peace, breathe
Take time. What is it that you want?
Envision that which will be best
Sometimes, the things we really strive for and
fight for have no need for you

The universe is crafting an open space that doesn't need
you to stress and press
Sometimes it's there laid out in front of you
Sometimes you don't see me
You run, that I don't catch and throw you away
Sometimes you run, and you don't know I'll keep chasing
you.
Easy love, what then?
All that is me is labelled 'Handle with Care'

"Diseased Poetry"

I have no special or 'wordy' words
Simple: I like you and you like me
Therefore, as the author of diseased poetry,
What can I say? Everything embodied by the boy makes me sway,
I keep it all to myself and watch my perfect prime mate play—
Every touch, every nerve alive to you.
I pretend to listen to every word you say
But in all truth, I remain busy
Entangled by every caress, and every breath on top and within you.
You're not listening to me, are you? he says.
How can I, when I've never seen anything as celestial as you?

"I don't love you like you do."
Have no expectation for feelings
One's feelings can feel exaggerated
There were no fireworks or a crazy euphoria—
That will come to you much later.
The picture painted is not true:
I am not the girl you drew.
In any case, the psychedelic prediction of me is solely seen
in a world in which both of us remain asleep.

All discretion is re-wired in a female brain;
The best advice cannot be taken for self.
I'll paint you a picture—
Man: Boy rejected; introduce common sense
Woman: Girl rejected; introduce delusional distress.

What is the female anatomy?
Creatures forever living in a lapsed reality.

"Sharp Words"

My mother always warned me about a man taking advantage,
Not emotionally or sexually
The not-so-common reality of a man disgusted:
He is on top, and I, the lower creature,
Awakened by events that did not go his way.
The path, the way he chose next, uncovered true colours
bewildering to me.
The boogie man under my bed!
The Scammer of Love!
My Father Christmas dressed up as my Valentine
on a low decline.
Self-disappointment turned on me,
Sharp words in direct penetration of me,
Is it clear that those vowels, symbols and 'doing'
words reflect me?
In pain, anguish, despair and all respect lost for me—
Love and all its bounty have been squared out.
No longer lovers, we have started a war.
On the defence, how can I forget?
The lair of your heart: all that is calloused is how you see me.
If spoken in pre-tense, how am I to put it in past tense?

"I sit in silence"

And I hear my thoughts more clearly,
Spectator of love, I now leak sense—
Sober in obscurity
Released from what ifs, whys and goodbyes—
I've never known solitude as the silence of absence,
Never known the presence of a man
To bring me to a place where I'm on my knees
Begging the stars for redemption,
Begging the heavens to take me.
If I cannot have you, my life is but a speck
Dirt irrelevant and useless
in rejection. I ask the next question—
With all the sun, moon and stars—
Cupid and all your mistresses of love, will you
Open the cleft of that which led me astray
Take away that which is beating
Wipe away the pumping love vessel?
Whatever the ending, I humbly accept its illusion.
For what is love but pain and misery
For what is love but a delight surely never meant for me?

"Mr Redding and Miss Glenda Devine"

Glenda, you walk with your head in the sky
Miss Glenda, I wish I was your vision
Conviction of connection
I feel it as my feet give way—
What kind of spell is she trying to give me?
Spoonful. Somebody walk in these arms of mine,
Sitting by the bayou, telling the lily pads
I'm chained to the love of Glenda Devine.
Sweat dripping on my forehead—
She's taking my strength—
Gripping the earth and all that's left of an old man's mind.
Tremble of a bass string
Quiver of tendons crying
Grieving words yet to be spoken
Body warmth of a hand not yet held
Dusty knees with a crazy man begging *please*
Tailored suit just to match your pretty
Escalating brass band playing the tune of a future at hand.
Miss Glenda . . . ?
With my perm, just right, it
Says I'm fine
Miss Glenda, instead of being Devine,
Darling, just say you'll be mine

"Me and my Pride"

Mind retains
Could we also turn back the things of beauty?
Could we masterminds turn back these times?
Make them better or add the spice of controversy
To bring him to his knees—
Apologies and employment under our ego.
Woman. Queen Bee. The higher power.
Not the equal lover.
Quiver
liver matured, caterpillars forming
Warm movements within, form the digestive system.
I miss you.
Thoughts outline a process to capture and
relive every moment.
Pride
Not enough to call
'Cause I'd rather suffer having you believe
I'm living better without you—
Truthfully knowing this world has lost its entirety without you.

"Man"

Manscape (escape)
Manstakes (mistakes)
Mantraits (traits)
Mantra
Caloundra, him and I
Lie for days
Sunrays and stingrays of love
Tentacles of commitment
Menstrual system
Bleeding of the heart
Hours upon hours focused on one scenario:
The mind strains and vertical atoms are
Wishing things turned out better

"Human"

He said I've found the one
He said I've found the human I cannot be without.
A pen, though in the dark, will find my thoughts on paper
So vast with love and faithfulness, she can only be a god.
I cannot lean on just understanding (I want some more)—
A human with the anatomy of a perfect love song
A human I see as the stars look down at me
in sure grace aligned
A human with a degree of a perfect summer
Sunshine, no restraint, she makes my heart content
A human who smiles just like my mother
A memory of the greatest woman I've loved
Reincarnated, I will continue to love

"Nights (Old Age)"

As the moon covers the night, remember me
As the light meets the dark, dance with me
As the wildlife comes alive, sing a song for me
As the ocean thunders to the shore,
Always return me.
As my feet walk the ocean floor,
Till the water sees my prints no more,
Remember the young girl you once fell for.
As the night sheltered me in the heavens above,
Remember you will be the one I always love.

"Stars together"

We once looked at the stars together—
Peered at the serenity and eclipse of wonders brought down to man.
How could I forget the wonder right next to me: man?
I've always loved the stars and all that they signify.
Abraham counted the stars with his God;
His descendants became as many as the sand on the shore.
Here I am, descended on the shore.
I look at the stars and I ask God
Could the person next to me forever be?
I do not ask for much although the man next to me holds an eternity. I forever worship, give praise and honour.
What is man that he should be alone?
What is man if not meant for Autumn alone?

"You"

"No fanciful aristocracy to explain all that is you.
Whispers in warm arms, leaves the question of
what would I do without you?
Ask me, what is my dream come true?
Simplistic terms, anything with you."

"Second Chance"

"Preciousness scattered graciously before me,
Oxygenated carbon dioxide plastered over me,
Re-enacted history working in favour of me,
Old Love returned to me."

"Hibernation"

I hibernated in the water
Words of others were my muse
I fell in love with another
Myself, she was called.

"Pride Part 2"

Customary tales come home
I'd never have believed I could be wrong—
Not that it's a problem in an equation of two.
I have my many disasters, it pains my pride to say so
Now that I've said so
The sorrows and my regrets
You've uncovered—my underlying layers—
Lie here with me.
Work out my grievances with grace
Love me with your love and watch me return to myself.

"Oh yeah"

I've always lived under the perception of past history,
Living out a life reincarnated by characters out of a book.
In the midst of it, I hadn't even met the real me.
Pictures of true love quotes
Plastered all over my wall
Images of what I'm supposed think to be me.
What I didn't know is
I was coming to know the real me
And what love was
reoccurring in a delusion.
Out of body and twenty,
Running into the arms of love and in search of
what its preciousness had for me.

"Hung out to dry"

Heart hung out to dry,
Callousness covers pure flesh.
Walls encompass theories of a lack of vulnerability.
I wear pride on my chest—
Watch me beat my chest
To not care, not share.
Daddy and Lover share a home,
You both take your coffee black and strong.
Soul, ditto—too strong to even hold a feeling.

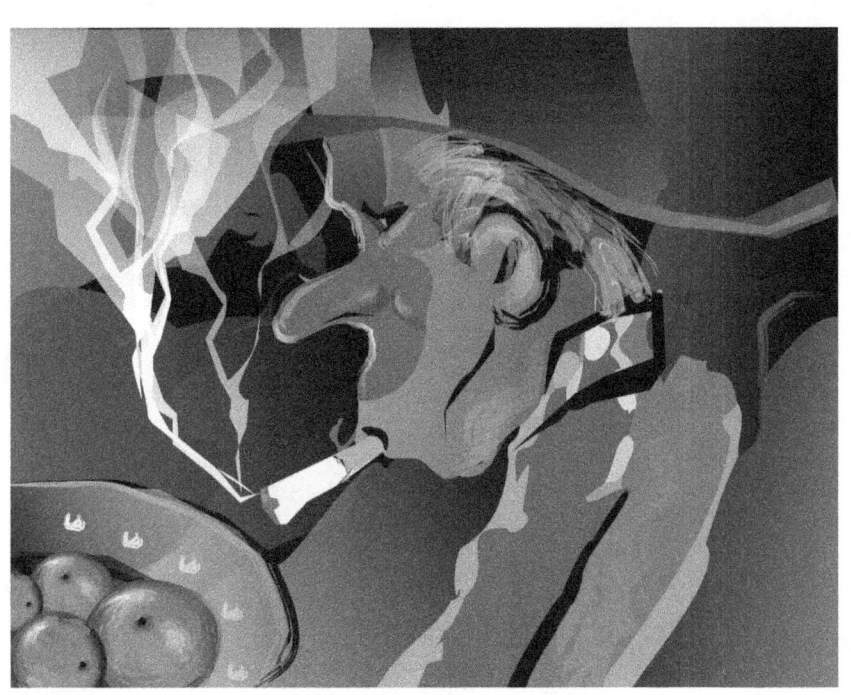

"Hello, Stranger"

Hello, stranger. Are you still awake?
Your eyes, no longer hollow
But welcomed home.
Warm your heart—
Fragments within self no longer contain contamination;
Bitterness, distress and anger:
You die a thousand deaths daily
Yet wake energised with a morning coffee.
You breathe words like you do love.
Nostalgia, damn your familiar face,
Commonly the roughest—
Get over it, I told you.
Bam, Baby, you're cured!
Ha.
Yet Memories still overtake you in the winter breeze,
Giddiness embraces you in the moments of remembrance.
I told ya, don't fall in Love
Stupid is what stupid does
And
All you do, Stupid, is fall in love.

"Kiss kiss"

7:24 Tyson Alerted: When do I get to kiss you?
7:48 The non-thirsty instant reply: The Altar.
Thus the end of him and I.
Kumbaya, quite the virgin, quite bizarre.
No commodities of first or second dates
Matrimony
Our lips in Harmony.
16, 17, 18, 19, 20—then he met me,
Knocked my socks off, then my vows went off,
Never to be a husband but ever the kisser.
A disappointment?
Never with two-dollar shared coffees in
between the esplanade.
Christmas Cheer—your first kiss is near!
Place, Handsome Boy, fireworks and one doorstop:
Out of the friend zone and into the kiss zone.

"Sweet spot"

Heartbreak, pain, the sweet sweet spot—
A residence I know all too well.
Always a metamorphosis of self-moulding
Seen with a knife carving out delicacies of the past
You need to change, the world tells me
I tell myself too . . . Yesterday's me is quite the bore.
Blonder, maybe? Stencil my skin a new arrangement
Bury old and awaken insecurities—
They wander in the cacoon
However, they don't stay long
Consisting and contributing to what they call a process.
I need change, I breathe change—
It calls my name and I will be subject to its requirements.
Old wine bursts, pouring into the new wine skin
Jacob's Creek in the presence of my enemies
I look in the mirror,
reflect on what I've made up in my makeup
Lies smudged in lines, lipsticked in the name of love.
Truth is I don't know what love is
I never have and I question what I have allowed myself to
be
Indecent, tearing, oversharing, self-destructive, capsizing,
overanalysing, daydreaming, disappointing, hand-holding,
stargazing, depressed, anxious, angry, in
Love.

Daddy would be so proud I found a man just like you.
Too much?
My daddy issues shine through my core—
No doctor needs to diagnose my constant need to love a man till he rejects me.
I've never finished anything on my own terms, seeking the same ending I found in my father,
Begging for the man I love to stay.
So I remain on my knees,
Waiting for the young man to become a daddy to me.
I can't write my own conclusion;
I grip mercilessness in its entirety.
Oh, the joy found in me
I pursue mental stability,
I drink myself into unconsciousness about truths I always knew.
But that's the funny thing:
Out the lips of another truth replicates into harsh realities.
I'm crazy, maybe a psychopath.
I find myself paralysed with Japanese beer,
Contaminating my blood stream
And all that I seem to care about is
Losing my best friend.

He's not such a bad person;
In all honesty, he was divine.
I'm lost in stupidity.
Let me tell ya, I wouldn't change a thing—
No, ma'am.
He gave me life before and after he left,
Softer yet wiser.
I want recompense. Give me his good,
But all divinity in heaven and karma (tastic) goodness.

I say these things because I care.
Fragile thoughts in the making, driving out the throbbing
in my heart.
Corny. I'll try again:
I want to make him feel the way he made me feel.
Tiredness is having the ghost of one's presence haunt
your thoughts when you're nothing but alone.
Silence. Time to sleep. Again to wake up love only when
desired. Until I am desired.

"Shepherd"

"Tested by every turn you make, wistful gentle breast, I lay my heavy head to rest, tender Shepherd leading sheep into green pastured love."

"Dear Elena"

Elena, I want to be like you
Elena, I know I am not you. That's okay.
I walk the streets with blondes and all he sees is you.
Blondes make me sick because when I'm with him, he wants you.
I live in your shadow and it's a cruel existence
He talks about you so much you and I are now practically best friends.
Sometimes I wish I was born before you, Sophia and whoever was before me.
Maybe then he'd have me tattoed on his chest
And you'd know how it feels to love a man who always sees you as second best.
I anoint myself with vanilla oils so my senses can drive your spirit away.
Nothing can break your and Rothman's tie.
He begs me day and night
To be inside me.
How can I, Rothman?
As far as I am concerned, my insides are just a sandpit compared to her wonderland.
You love her and not me
My insides are the only thing I have left.
He stares at breasts and thighs that make me feel less then alive.

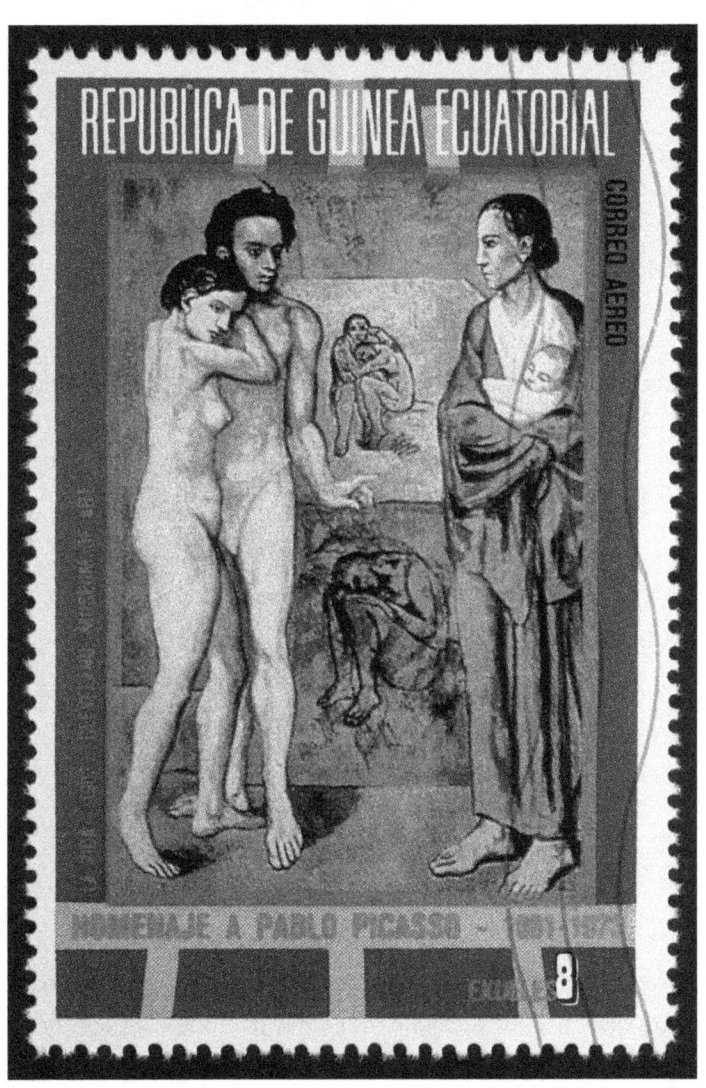

And when he's with me
He cries, Deprived.
It's okay, he tells me, my sisters don't believe in free love
either.
But I want to make you feel good
Without commitment. I cry No—
Left in bed, wounded, as he leaves.
Neither of us left with what we wanted.
So there I lie in bed,
Insides intact but heart sexed, hit and quitted.
Let me ask you, Elena, now that we are acquainted and
have shared the same cigarette,

Would you yourself have given all yourself to be a
conquest, second best and never to be loved?
Help me, for I am naïve and in love,
I fear I have no choice but to give him back to you.
Do as you please.
He will come back to you,
But this time with a piece of my heart.
Could you scatter the ashes and lay them to rest?
My life depends on it.
I end on this: that I desired to be you
but it could never be.
If I was you, my entirety would belong to you and no man,
my dear friend, should reduce me to nonexistence, no
matter how well I love him.

"Every smell I smell him"

Every Smell I smell him
Every Breeze his caress.
Just like the wind, his presence felt but quiet,
Demanding and yet so unaware.
In Fire, I see him—
Fixed gaze and consuming everything within me.
He was an array of songs written just for me,
All things whole and delicious and on cold nights
depressingly foul.
Do you remember your awkward laugh?
Of course you do—
Ha—and you were done
Ha—and I was in love, done.
Crazy simplistic,
I like that about you.
Your laugh brought a touch of innocence,
A little squint of the little boy inside caught by his parents
being naughty, so mad but a look so sweet, you couldn't
help but not be angry.
That was you and me, sweet innocent boy,
A mommy of a girl who couldn't but forgive you anyway.
I've got these hectic beats I want you to hear,
lovely boy. Let's cascade into disaster one more time.

"Sweet solitude"

Dear friend of mine,
Speak of no words
But thoughts heard aloud—
My tears for your ear.
No one is here
That's how you like it
Party of one
Loneliness has no one.
I look in the mirror
Veins across my eyes
Mixed with salt and hopeless hope
Mascara pouring forth.
Does this world have much worth?
Jump off a balcony
But you'll get the best of me—
How would that feel?
Kill pain with another pain:
Staying alive to feel even worse pain

"Take me to your river"

Sweet nicotine kisses,
Take me to your river.
Love enters, reality disappears.
Are your waters nice this year?
I enter your paths and I am refreshed,
Laughter and warmth fill my cheeks.
I wanna set by your streams after fifty.
I like fishies and you.
What are your reeds like?
I'll bathe in your affection
And you'll be my protection.
Let's go fishing.
Can I reel out your goodies
And you catch my bait of *I love yous*?
Will I come today and see you blue,
Cold and undesirable?
Take me to your river—
Let me go in your depths,
Splash you back to life,
Warm you with my body heat,
Let you forget what it's like to be alone.
Take me to your river,
Let me lie in your streams
Till I'm wrinkled and old.
Take me to your river
Till I can take no more.

"Perception"

Expose weakness,
Flaws and darkness—
Myself I hide.
Perfect I want to be in your perception.
Interruption—true colours
Hiding, but invisible invitations for acceptation and to relent.
I am enamoured with how I want you to view me:
Passed out on the grass,
Never a bad thought of you, am I led astray?
Although one moon left me dismayed—
Alcohol became your lover that night,
Took you to bed and embodied your blood stream.
Further then we've been
Jealous
The stars tell a different tale:
Pinocchio
Sad Boy
Not a real Man
Figment of my imagination
Claiming fleshly ways
But all that was there was wood.
The night winds holds my arms

As I'm tempted to fly away.
Marina Mirage and nostalgia go hand in hand:
Mind plays tales searching for a soaring epitome,
What I hope will happen.
Miss yous have feelings
Yet no love.
What BS.
What form of nature are you that you should return,
Faltered and a dent to society,
Hurting so mathematically you hurt others?
Perfect mayhem.
I do believe, sir, you are incorrect mathematically.
My mind is in arrears in what the fairy tales
Should've given me.
Self. I am now
Again the strain, filling an empty vessel,
All to be poured out again.
Can I pour out again?
I read books of knowledge,
Learning to love myself again.
Who am I again?
Taken over by another, I have lost sense of self.
I rarely want to be alone with myself,
I am a stranger to myself—.
Boring and damaged.
No wants to play with baggage,
No one goes on holiday to return unpacking ruins of
returning back to reality.

Stephen returned to New York.
I wonder what he was in search of—
Was he tired of life on the coast, his soul left not at rest?
He got me or was it a ploy to be the other man?
Are you two still together?
Was it concern or an invitation shared between the joint
and Asahis at his joint?
We came for different reasons—
I came for my passport,
He came for love.
I got mine,
And, well, he had a beer.
Never ever have I been disappointed by a beer.
That was my parting gift.
No stress—you'll find a good grown woman
Who loves red wine and takeaway as much as you do,
A lady who doesn't mind her whiskey warm with no ice.
You never had ice.
I noticed, yes.
I wish I could've given him answers that he searched for;
I know how desperately one can be in need of those.
Maybe he isn't even bothered.
These are just the thoughts in my head.
I'd tell him
My profession took our buddy time;
I'm sorry I didn't come to your birthday party;

Happy birthday, Homie;
Your laugh is contagious and your company warm as
homes should be;
You're the better man who just can't be mine.
It's kind of hard when you love another ass of a man.

I should apologise to you too, Josh,
My Isle of Man man.
Without you, the show wouldn't have gone on.
I'm still deciding if that's good or bad.
I became your friend to take your best friend.
I let you put on my anklet as a sign of ownership
To show him I wanted to own him too.
Drunken karaoke and guessing games were so fun.
Behind it all, I wanted those exact things with another man—
Right there in your living room—
Just without you.

"How I love Love"

How I love love—
Love in unconditional form
Love in its hardest form.
Whether or not they loved me or not,
I knew I loved them,
And that was love
As long as I was in it.
It was just that
Love holds no record of wrongs
So I forgot wrongs
Saw them in their purest forms
Voices said *you were cruel*
Love whispered *you were true*
Love told me you were hurt so you hurt others.
I knew how to heal you and hurt myself at the same time—
A slave by the stove to show I cared,
A slave to show I cared.
Music was our playground;
Hand in hand, we whisked away all our inhibitions of any
right judgement.

My peculiar treasure,
I see you.
So much gold.
You were my
Midnight kiss
Shooting star wish
Salty rain
Heavy kisses
My adventure
My man with a fast-approaching beer belly
My obsession
Man in uniform
Mean face
All-serious, timeless soul
Golden skin
Green-eyed elixir
I want to drink all of you till you're empty.

Let's have a do-over:
Text me *Hey*
Swim in Labrador again
Shut me up with kisses
Make me weak in the knees with your Americanese
Dedicate wine bottles to you and me
Tickle me fancy with your golden beard
I'm need of your love.
I love you, love.

"Thoughts"

Let go of the things that don't want you:
The world gives you hints of desire and
everything barbed wire.
What lies behind your kind eyes?
I want the pain to be self-destructing
I want beauty for ashes
Resurrect the Lazarus within me—
I am far too dense.

"Daddy, put my soul to rest"

Pitter-patter, shit-shatter my heart goes.
In the solitude, literal insanity faces my soul.
I hear depression call my name
And, Mercy, say no!
Your bright eyes bring life to this carcass. I see you and me waltzing in an awkward attempt of you drawing me back to your heart and my constantly fleeing from your rest.
I chase dreamy eyes, crazy dreams, feelings and utter regret.
Yeah, I'm a total loser.
Stupid girl calls your name, heartbroken again,
And there you are, perfect and all.
Daddy, honestly, how could you look at me with such love?
Daddy, you put my soul at rest.
Even though the fear of losing out on love won't let me rest,
You give and you take away.
The door of my heart falls desperately at the heels of your feet
In search of a miracle.
Yet I don't want to be alone tonight.
I can still smell his scent—the loneliness suffocates my

chest—
The loneliness driving my feet straight to his door and
choosing less than the best.

In pursuit, I see the way he unravels me,
Gentle to the touch but harsh to my soul.
His sheep's clothing masks my weary emotions.
The wolf I willingly invited in
And all I can say to you, my maker, is I'm sorry,
Please love me, I beg, satisfy me.
Sometimes, Daddy, emptiness jumps into my soul,
Fear leads me to forget you.

I don't know what to do, I don't do the things I want to,
But the things I don't want to do, I do.
I close the door to my heart
And I fall at your feet—
Ground me
Surround me
Change me
Mould me
Fill me with your presence so I know I'm not alone
Put my heart to rest with time
Help me to give you my all to rest.

Most of all, Daddy, would you put my broken past lover's
soul to rest.

Today I'm going to smoke my life away.
Do not ponder me;
Take me as I am.
Invite me to your missionaries—
I still dwell to worship,
I fight to conquer the demons that wrestle me,
I strain to think about what will bring me pleasure.
A shadow of what I've lost and still cannot contain,
A temple that is for worship,
Clouded by smoke and in constant need of my saviour.
How I wish I could share these thoughts with you.
I fear that I may be rejected as before.
There was a time I was my perfect self—
Holy and true just for you,
The perfect façade
However empty and in despair.
I saw my mentor in the playground of hell.
He was what I longed for, to be close with God,
And a god subtly.
We cannot share those thoughts.
Here are mine.
I know these thoughts will not be accepted as I once was.
I am angry at the church,
I want God and not its people—
They are as the world described:
Hypocritical and priests that touch boys.

What I know now is that, that is what they are:
Just people.
Imperfections of a true God.
It still hurts, knowing truth.
Here's an idea:
I'll smoke my life away
To take me far from my worries,
Make me feel I'm an artist like Frida.
But once the butt is gone,
All sensation is gone.
My soul cries out as I desecrate my temple—
And there is God
In the midst of my worries, highlighted bright.
You're human, but it's not an excuse.
It does not bring hope or triumph.
I am destroying me,
A pawn for the world to see,
A hypocritical Christian,
A representation of love.
What is my answer?

www.ingramcontent.com/pod-product-compliance
Lightning Source LLC
Chambersburg PA
CBHW020022050426
42450CB00005B/593